BUILDING MENTAL STRENGTH FOR SUCCESS

A Powerful Book To Activate Winning Mindset, Boost Confidence, Conquer Challenges And Become Mega Successful In Life.

PRADIP N DAS

Contents

Introduction

"The ability to continue moving when you are feeling scared, fearful or lazy is the sign of true mental strength." – Matthew Donnelly

One day Thomas Edison came home from school and gave a paper to his mother. He told her, "My teacher gave this paper to me and told me explicitly to give it to my mother."

His mother's eyes were tearful as she read the letter out loud to her child, "Your son is a genius. This school is too small for him and doesn't have enough good teachers for training him. Please teach him yourself."

After many years, he was now one of the greatest inventors of the century. After Edison's mother died, one day, he was looking through old family things. Suddenly he saw a folded paper in the corner of a drawer in a desk. He took it and opened it up. On the paper was written, “Your son is addled. We won’t let him come to school anymore.”

That day, Edison cried for hours, and then he wrote in his diary, “Thomas Alva Edison was an addled child that, by a hero mother, became the genius of the century.”

Achievers and high performers from all walks of life face ups and downs along the path to success—they face failure, burnout, discouragement, fatigue, self-limiting beliefs, stress, and so much more.

How do some people continually strive towards their personal goals year after year while others give up on them? How do those people stay strong and persevere when there is so much stacked against them?

At its core, mental strength is simply the ability to stick to something when the going gets tough. People with high levels of mental strength can push beyond these obstacles and forge a path towards success, while those with lower levels of mental toughness may abandon their dreams.

Life is everything but a bed of roses. Numerous ups and downs drive life, and they characterize our intensity of mental strength. This book has covered the basic understanding of Mental Strength, its role in success, benefits of mental strength and finally the Methods to improve the mental strength. Building Mental Strength for Success is suitable not just for beginners but also for those who have encountered a stagnant roadblock in professional or personal life.

Understanding Mental Strength

"The ability to continue moving when you are feeling scared, fearful or lazy is the sign of true mental strength." – Matthew Donnelly

What is Mental Strength?

Everyone wants to achieve tremendous success in their life. But we can all agree that achieving success can be difficult no matter what your ambitions are, and it requires a daily grind for a more extended period, which takes a toll on physical, mental, and emotional energy.

Mental strength is the ability of an individual to effectively deal with challenges, pressure, and stressors to present their best performance regardless of the circumstances. Mental strength requires you to balance your emotions and rational thinking to work together to make informed decisions that guide your behavior.

Mental strength, often called mental toughness, is essential for business, sports, relationships, and every aspect of life. You have to be mentally strong to work through problems, find solutions, and keep pushing yourself forward. In other words, improving your mental strength should be of utmost priority for one to live a happier and more successful life.

Mental Strength is the individual capacity to deal effectively with stress, challenges, and pressure to perform to the best of their ability, irrespective of the circumstances.

Building mental strength is fundamental to living a good life in terms of meaningful social life, positive self-esteem, coping with difficult situations, and taking risks at different life points.

Everyone possesses mental strength to some degree, but there is always scope for improvement. The greater the mental strength, the healthier and stronger you will become, and the more likely you are to reach your goals, experience more joy, happiness, and satisfaction in life.

Mental toughness is a developed skill that allows a person to push through difficult circumstances without losing confidence and performing the best during challenging situations.

Role Of Mental Strength In Success

Success is fifty percent in mind. Whether your goal is to become a great leader, a sports champion, a prosperous entrepreneur, or an efficient professional, mental strength plays a crucial role in long-term success. You are not born with mental strength, but rather it is a skill that you learn and develops during the journey of life. Like physical strength, some people could have more mental toughness based on knowledge, skills, experiences, and personality.

Mental strength is the ability of an individual to deal with challenges, pressure effectively, and stresses to present their best performance regardless of the circumstances. Mental strength requires you to balance your emotions and rational thinking to work together to make informed decisions that guide your behavior.

To have mental strength means you are aware of emotions and thoughts and work concurrently with them to choose your actions. In other words, mental strength is about responding, not reacting.

You will always encounter challenges and obstacles in life that stand in your way, but with mental strength, you develop resilience to those threats and have the strength to continue on your success journey.

Mental strength, often called mental toughness, is essential for attaining success in business, sports, relationships, and every aspect of life. You have to be mentally strong to work through problems, find solutions, and keep pushing yourself forward. In other words, improving your mental strength is the number one thing you can do to live a happier and more successful life. Mental strength is needed to compete at the highest level and to achieve one's maximum potential.

Mental Strength is the ability of a person to deal productively with the challenges, roadblocks, and pressures they experience in business and life. Having mental strength requires commitment, consistency in performing positive daily habits to make daily progress despite setbacks and failures.

Mentally strong people do not bother about their thought process, do not compare themselves to others, and take on challenges headlong irrespective of their capability. Building this mental toughness increases confidence and self-esteem and allows us to take on more significant challenges despite a fear of failure.

Having mental strength allows people to take risks, take on new challenges, and cope with difficult situations and experiences. People with mental strength focus on the positives in their life and surround themselves with other people who are also mentally healthy.

Can Mental Strength Be Learned?

Like any other skill, mental strength is a learnable skill. You learn notes to learn singing; you learn steps to learn dancing.

Similarly, you need to learn some methods to acquire mental strength.

Like physical strength or building muscle, mental strength is available to every person to a certain degree. The physical strength of a person improves when they do physical exercises and practices every day. So when you are developing your mental strength, you need to realize that the process is the same as physical strength and does not happen overnight. Still, slowly, you can develop by proper training, taking daily actions, and having patience. Mental strength is developed over time when you choose to be courageous and committed to your self-development. By practicing daily gratitude, focusing on abundance, and developing resilience, people with mental toughness choose to live their life on their terms. Mentally strong individuals overcome setbacks with confidence simply because adversities make them better.

Improve Courage

"Be brave. Take risks. Nothing can substitute experience." –Paulo Coelho

One cowardly person comes to learn martial arts. The master looked at him and said,

"I will teach you only on one condition that you will have to stay in the city for one month. There you have to tell every person you meet on your way that you are a coward. You will have to say it loudly, openly, and looking straight into the person's eyes."

On hearing this, the person got very sad, because he felt it was scary to say that he is a coward loudly. For a couple of days, he was sorrowful and kept on contemplating, but to live with his cowardice was unbearable for him. So, he decided to travel to the city to accomplish his mission.

At first, when he met somebody, he trembled, lost his speech, and couldn't speak to anyone. But he needed to finish the task, so he kept on trying to overcome this fear. When he talked to his first passer to tell about his cowardice, it seemed to him that he would die. Slowly, he gained confidence, and his voice sounded louder and more confident with every passing day. Suddenly came a moment when the person caught himself thinking that he is not scared anymore, and the further he continued doing the master's task, the more convinced he was that the fear had vanished. That way, a month had passed.

The person returned to the master, bowed to him, and said, "Thank you, teacher. I finished your task. Now I am not afraid anymore. But how did you know that this strange task will help me?"

The thing is that cowardice is only a habit. When we do the things that scare us, we can destroy the stereotypes and nip the fear at its bud. And now you know that bravery is also a habit. And if you want to make bravery a part of yourself, you need to immerse yourself in the fear. Then the fear will go away, and courage will take its place.

What Is Courage?

High mental strength people also prefer to learn from the mistake and move on. They always think about bouncing back with full strength. When they think about bounce back, they are also ready to take a certain risk level to come back. This requires courage. Courage is nothing but the power to take the risk.

When we hear the word courage, we generally visualize scenarios around defending from an attack. The attack can be physical, verbal, emotional, or psychological. Yet, a sign of individual courage is not just defending an attack, but when triggered, it can have significant positive benefits for our health and wellbeing, opportunities for success, and our ability to move forward from the crisis.

Courage can be physical, moral, and psychological courage. Physical courage is generally defined as the kind of courage we draw upon when facing a physical threat. It relies on us to put our physical selves at risk to protect ourselves or others from bodily harm or assault. On the other hand, moral courage is the type of courage we need when we must stand up to a social wrong or social hypocrisy and is the kind of courage most often represented in stories and fables. It relies on us risking our social standing and our peers' support but is embedded in our values and sense of right and wrong. Psychological courage refers to the strength we have to confront the truth of ourselves and our behaviors and to act where required to elicit change. It is the kind of courage needed to acknowledge and accept the dissonance or gap that may exist between who we think we are and who we are.

It takes courage to step outside of your comfort zone and face your fears head-on. After all, there's no guarantee that the risks you'll take will turn out the way you want.

Courage is developed in many ways, like taking actions, taking calculated risks, keeping in uncomfortable positions, making mistakes.

If a person keeps taking action, he can anticipate the consequences; he can take a calculated risk, accept failures, accept changes. It brings a lot of pain and discomfort to the person but gradually develops all the qualities required for success, including courage.

Courage is not the absence of fear. Courageous people feel fear, but they can manage and overcome their fear to not stop them from taking action.

They often use the fear to ensure that they are not overly confident and take the appropriate actions.

Suppose a bird is sitting on the top branch of the tall tree, enjoying the view from the branch. Even if a strong wind started blowing, and the tree swayed with high intensity, the bird would not be worried.

The bird was not worried for two crucial reasons. The first, even without the branch, it can fly and thus remain safe through the power of its own two wings. The second, it also knew that there were many other branches upon which it can sit.

This small story tells us a lot about our own self-confidence and courage. Throughout our own lives, there are many so-called branches and trees on which we rely on. And while sometimes we do need recovery and shelter, as we grow, we also learn that these sources of safety do not always last – what is lasting and permanent rests within us, in the form of positive self-esteem and belief in our unique abilities.

Help To Bounce Back

"Winners are not afraid of losing. But losers are. Failure is part of the process of success. People who avoid failure also avoid success."
– Robert T. Kiyosaki

Thomas Alva Edison is famous for two things. First, he invented the light bulb. Second, he is known for famously having said, "I haven't failed. I have just found 10,000 ways that won't work." Edison is one of the first people who paid more attention to his journey than his success at the end of the road. In our childhood, we heard this quote many times that it is the journey that is important. However, as we grow old, we forget to focus on the things that matter; instead, we often look only at results.

Success meets lots of failures on the way. Some people can quickly bounce back, while others find it difficult during failures or at the time of setbacks.

Striving for success is healthy, but believing that you will succeed the first time may not always work. Mentally strong people believe that failure is part of the process toward a long journey to success. By viewing failure as a temporary setback, they are able to bounce back and move forward with ease.

Mentally healthy people are in control of their thoughts, feelings, emotions, and behaviors. They are always ready to cope up with life's challenges. They can keep problems in perspective and bounce back from setbacks. Failure is always painful. Sometimes, it can feel impossible to bounce back. But recovering from a setback can make us feel proud and instill in us a sense of confidence and self-reliance.

Can Bounce Back Be Possible?

When life meets failure, are you quick to stand yourself up and get back to the task? Or do you find yourself completely overwhelmed with little confidence in your ability to deal with the challenge?

But there is no need to worry as many practical strategies are available for building mental resilience. So, you need to learn those strategies and practice those with discipline and hard work.

Our resilience is often tested when unexpected challenges arrive; however, it allows rising above and coming back even more potent than you were before.

Read on to learn techniques to build and improve your mental resilience and deal effectively with life's challenges.

Bouncing back is certainly possible, but it depends on the person’s present mindset. If he is overwhelmed by the circumstances and completely upset mentally, and negative thinking has taken him over, then it is an uphill task to come back. The role of mental strength comes into the picture at that time. The stronger the mental strength, the quicker he will be able to get around.

How Successful People Bounce Back

One of the crucial traits of highly successful people is that they have the perseverance to bounce back from failure quickly. While for other people, failure becomes a permanent roadblock between them and success. However, mentally strong people see setbacks as an opportunity to upgrade themselves, sharpen their skills, and become better at what they do. Here is how mentally strong people turn setbacks into comebacks:-

- Create a plan: Mentally strong people view failure as an inevitable part of the long journey to success. They turn each setback into a scope of improvement by reviewing what went wrong, gathering more information, and after that creating a new action plan.

- Practice self-compassion: Rather than repenting for the mistake, mentally strong people do self-talk and understand the situation in-depth. They speak to themselves with kind and supportive words of encouragement.

- Respect their weaknesses: Mentally strong people use failure as an opportunity to spot their weaknesses. They always try to be realistic, accept their shortcomings and mistakes, never trying to hide them. They always remain humble and make strategies to become a better person.

- Take failure in the right perspective: Mentally strong people do not get overly upset when things do not go as per their plan. Instead, they take setbacks in the right perspective. They channelize their thoughts positively and adequately manage their emotions to continue behaving productively during the hardship.

- Practice gratefulness: Mentally strong people choose to be grateful for opportunities to try new things. They always search for the silver lining. Their willingness to look for the silver lining keeps their positivity alive as they decide to move forward.

- Acknowledge their strengths: Mentally strong people acknowledge their positive attributes without arrogance and evaluate their strengths. They recognize what they do well so they can build upon these existing strengths.

- Maintain a healthy self-worth: As long as they behave according to their values, mentally strong people feel good about themselves, regardless of their personal or professional failures. Their confidence helps them to find the courage to get back up each time they fall.

Boost Confidence

Inaction breeds doubt and fear. Action breeds confidence and courage. If you want to conquer fear, do not sit home and think about it. Go out and get busy." - Dale Camegie

As rightly described by one of the Buddhist sayings, 'Every battle is won before it is fought.' Before actually facing a problem, in our mind, we decide the outcome.

Samir was a below-average student in studies. He was always under pressure because he belongs to a middle-class Indian family where parents think studying is the only way to excel in life. Till 10th grade, he somehow managed to pass examinations, but he was losing hope; he was fearful about the future because all he knew was academic excellence is what you need to succeed in life.

His mental strength was fragile because he had never worked on it. After his 10th exams, one day, he was sitting with his grandfather in a playground. His grandfather was good at reading minds. He knew what he was going through. He tried to help him out at times, but he was so surrounded by negatives that he couldn't help. That day Samir was sitting clueless; his grandfather put his hand on his head and said, “You have immense potential, you are fearless, don’t try to fit in where you don’t belong to. You can achieve anything you want. Just give your best shot, don’t take life personally; it shouldn't be taken in that way. Do whatever you want to. Search for your passion. People will always have something to say, don’t care about them. You are fearless, be fearless.”

That word fearless stuck in his head tightly. He looked at him; he was so calm like still water, so beautifully he described the meaning of this life. He came back home, that night he couldn't sleep. He was so right; he was trying to fit in where he doesn't belong.

He loved science very much, especially mathematics, physics, and chemistry but couldn't fit well in the school system. The next day he told his father that he wants to move to Kota to take coaching classes for IIT JEE. He was shocked to hear that, but he convinced him. During the course journey, there were moments when he thought of giving up, but he had promised that he would give his best shot, and he did. On one fine day, the result came out, and he had achieved All India Rank 423 and got admission into IIT Delhi.

Self-confidence is your belief in your abilities, qualities, and judgments. Self-confidence and mental toughness are close blood relatives. For instance, when you are not mentally strong enough, you will question your ability to perform well in any situation. For example, if you have a speech to deliver, you will panic under pressure and probably make a fool of yourself in front of the audience. This affects your self-confidence, and you end up delivering a shallow speech because you broke under pressure. If, on the other hand, if you are mentally tough, you will not panic under pressure, and you will have faith in your ability to deliver a killer speech. Continually working on building your mental toughness increases your overall self-confidence at work, home, or in life. Moreover, when you are mentally tough, you quickly overcome past mistakes and failures. It allows you to build your confidence because you avoid lingering on mistakes long enough for them to damage your self-belief.

Confidence gives us the power to act on our convictions, have faith in ourselves or others, and take action. Over-confidence; can be costly when we may be too ready to take action and take unnecessary risks. Confidence is considered one of the most important attributes a person can have, yet it is also considered one of the most fragile characteristics. Therefore, finding ways to build and maintain confidence is essential for mental toughness development and successful performance.

While healthy amounts of self-confidence are helpful, overestimating your abilities can leave you ill-prepared for the realities of a challenge. Similarly, underestimating the time and energy, it will take to reach your goals can lead to disappointment. Mental strength is about recognizing shortcomings and acknowledging the hard work needed to reach a goal.

Courage And Self-Confidence

Courage and Self Confidence go hand in hand. Courage, in the present context, refers to the capacity of being able to follow your heart despite the opposition or difficulties involved. Fear is the principal adversary of self-confidence and fulfillment. With courage, you overcome all your limitations and fears to follow your achieved targets. This inevitably increases the possibility of your success. Self-confidence and courage give you the power to write your own destiny.

To build courage or restore your lost confidence, try to spend leisure time with friends, family, and dear ones. They will make you feel protected and will stand with you in every decision you make. This will undoubtedly lift your confidence and make you feel good about your life.

Confidence Is The Key To Success

Self Confidence is the key to success, or we can say the first step to success. If a person has self-confidence, he has won half the battle. Those people who have self-confidence at work, school, and daily life always appear on the top rung of the world. Everything seems to go right for these people, and they always seem to present themselves as calm, collected, and successful in everything they do.

Self-confident people understand the impact of believing in themselves and relying on their abilities.

Some people have so much confidence that they are not afraid to do anything. Others are the complete opposite and are scared of being judged or ridiculed by others. Self-confidence cannot be taught but is gained by the individual when they decide to believe in themselves. To attain self-confidence, one needs to believe that they can do the task at hand. It cannot be accomplished overnight but slowly gets stronger and stronger over a while. One of the significant ways to obtain confidence is acting confidently, even when not. Acting will transfer into truly being self-confident and having high self-esteem. Another way to gain confidence is by talking to others. My example of gaining confidence is a true testament that this works. Talking to people who care will lift one's spirit by talking about their excellent skills and immediately boosting confidence.

This confidence ultimately creates opportunities for success, and with each new success, another self-confidence building block is put into place. Success builds self-confidence with each new achievement. Self-confident people perceive themselves as able to achieve those things they set out to do, and this perception creates reality in their lives.

Yes, perception creates reality. You can become the person you want to be. You must have heard the saying that if you can believe it, you can achieve it.

So, start believing in yourself, act on that belief, and you will begin building self-confidence in your life. Building self-confidence needs specific steps to be followed.

Make a list of your strong points. Note down all the positive things about yourself and the things that you are good at doing. Think of compliments you have received or things that come quickly to you. It doesn't matter what it is; if it's useful, write it down.

Remember the times when you exhibited self-confidence and how good it felt. Keep trying again, and each time will help you build confidence, and finally, confidence-building will become a way of life. Success will automatically be achieved once you start believing in yourself.

How Mental Strength Increases Courage And Confidence?

Confidence may only last when you keep getting good outcomes. Mental strength is what is believed needed to maintain confidence to grow and achieve goals.

Constant working on building your mental toughness increases your overall self-confidence at work, home, or life. Moreover, when you are mentally tough, you quickly overcome past mistakes and failures. It allows you to build your confidence because you avoid lingering on mistakes long enough for them to damage your self-belief.

In conclusion, confidence is a characteristic that everyone struggles with at one point but can be achieved by trusting one's abilities and speaking with others that are supportive. Mark Twain once said, "The worst loneliness is not to be comfortable with yourself." Being comfortable in one's own skin is the key to achievement and enjoyment in life, starting with confidence.

Improve Perseverance

"Many of life's failures are people who did not realize how close they were to success when they gave up." –Thomas Edison

One day, a student seeks advice from his coach.

"Sir, I can't do this anymore," he said. "Those assignments only exhaust me, and the result remains the same." I am not destined to become a Grand Master in Chess, and my dream will never come true.

The coach looked at his student with loving eyes and said, "You know, every person in life has a dream, a goal of his life. The goals are the ones that push us to do what we are doing." He continues, "We have to fight for what we believe in, what we feel, what we desire. In other cases, you will be directionless. Once and for all."

The coach explained, “The easiest way is to quit everything because the path is difficult and we are not used to the inconveniences. We want everything to be easy, smooth at once. We become impatient. This is how our dream dies, and the goal becomes unreachable.”

Gradually, life becomes a routine without depth and meaning. Then one day, we try to forget and start everything from a new beginning; we wait for a new day to make our life different. But new obstacles come in our way, and we stop again. We are filled with despair and anger for our own helplessness.

But you only need to remember one thing: never give up, fight, battle. It doesn’t matter that you have lost one battle and even dozens of battles. Life goes on! Your biggest enemies are hiding in you – laziness, fear, doubt, indecision. Be a warrior of your dream, a knight of your goal, and a soldier of your wishes!

Mental Strength Pushes You To Persevere

We used to debate who was the most outstanding player - Pele or Maradona in Soccer, Serena Williams or Steffi Graf in Women Tennis, Brian Lara or Sachin Tendulkar in Cricket?

But in swimming, there is no debate. Michael Phelps is the only one name; he is the most excellent swimmer and most decorated Olympian of all times. He has won 28 medals over four different Olympic Games, 23 of them gold.

Michael Phelps said in an interview, "One of the craziest things my coach got me to do when we first started to train together was not to say the word 'can't.' It helped me broaden my mind and believe that I could do whatever I wanted to. And I think that was a key to us being so successful."

One of the critical features of Michael Phelps's training was "Visualization." In addition to a grueling training regimen that saw him spending hours in the pool seven days a week, he used to picture himself doing races the way he wanted. These two helped him to fine-tune his technique.

Michael Phelps could not have created history if he had not been working hard during days and nights over the years with tremendous perseverance. Had he not been persevering, Usain Bolt could not become the World's fastest sprinter by winning three gold medals in three consecutive Olympics.

Motivation comes and goes. But mentally stronger people helps you keep moving long after your desire to press on has disappeared.

It allows you to dig deep when you're tired or when you lack ambition. It helps you talk back to your brain when your brain tries to convince you to quit. Growing stronger ensures you will persist even when you do not feel like it.

On the path to success, you are going to run into a few roadblocks. The key is not a matter of avoiding these roadblocks as it continues despite these roadblocks. One of the keys to persevering despite setbacks is to develop mental toughness. If you are looking to develop mental toughness, there are several things you should do.

How Mental Strengths Improve Perseverance

Perseverance is nothing but habit and mental attitude, which requires mental toughness to translate your desires into actions. Grit and determination play a vital role in perseverance. To deal with discouragement, you need to remind yourself of your big dream and vision of why you decided to pursue this journey.

When a kid learns to stand up and walk, he keeps falling again and again. By nature and instinct, he gets up and again tries to step forward, and he falls again. But finally, he succeeds in walking. The same thing happened to each one of us when we were kids.

Perseverance is one of the essential secrets and the root cause of success. Perseverance is to keep on going during setbacks and challenges. It is the inner call of a human being to continue in the game when the entire environment says it's time to quit. It is just resolving to one foot after another when the finish line is nowhere in sight.

Mentally weaker people practice perseverance for a short period; their journey ends by giving up after trying for some time. But for mentally strong people, the period is more extended, over several years or even decades continues even after several failures. These are painful and testing moments where no matter how much effort you put in the journey, there is hardly any positive movement. Naturally, you will get discouraged thinking about what is going on; even more frustrating when you find out others around you are making good progress on their goals. But the question arises—how to keep on going? How to motivate ourselves when we get very thirsty by walking in the desert, and there is no water in sight?

Always remember that most successful people have endured hardships, challenges, and failures at some point in their life. They kept going because they kept their purpose and goals in mind, so they were determined to make a difference in both their lives and those of others.

Improve Ones' Ability To Learn From Mistakes

"When you make a mistake, there are only three things you should ever do about it: admit it, learn from it, and don't repeat it." - *Paul Bear Bryant*

At the time of any mistake, many of us try to find an excuse to justify our actions to escape the feeling of guilt, uncomfortable emotions, like disappointment and embarrassment. This discomfort can cause many people to give up on their goals after they fail. If we justify our mistakes to lessen our guilt, it sets us on the path of repeating them. Mental strength gives you the ability to take responsibility and acknowledge your mistakes. Admitting that you were wrong will help you avoid making the same mistake in the future, which is a valuable lesson that is crucial to grow and succeed.

Becoming mentally stronger will help you to bounce back from failure much quickly. This is how people become successful as they know that failure is part of the journey to success.

High mental strength people develop certain qualities in them like practicing a positive attitude, take the thing sportingly, and learn from that situation and move on.

Mental strength is the pillar on which the person is standing. The weaker the pillar, the weaker the building will be. Wherever there are earthquake-like tough challenges, the building will fall, or the person will crumble, can't withstand the pressure, and ultimately go down. Mental strength actually grows with learning and practice. Whenever any adverse situation happens, people should take it sportingly and courageously, deep think on why this happened, the learnings, what best we can do to avoid in the future, and more. When a person's mindset works in that direction, it will ultimately help them learn from the failure and march toward the goal.

High mental strength people have the courage and the mindset to take the situation as a part of the game and not taking as an abnormality.

Time and experience have proved to be the best teachers ever to exist. Failures are the stepping stones to success. Those mistakes make us a better person and strive hard to help us achieve our dream destination. Our mistakes teach us what went wrong and how to correct it. Every wrong or bad decision we take has a life lesson that we learn. Time is a way of telling how far you have come. Experience is a way of telling how strong you have become. We need to learn from the mistakes that we make.

Einstein once mentioned, "Anyone who has never made a mistake has never tried anything new." We can completely agree with this great mathematician's statement. It is the new experience and new exposures that teach you new things. With every new fall, you learn something new. If you are not ready to let yourself fall, then you cannot teach yourself anything new.

It's also important not to dismiss failure without any introspection. Failures can only teach us something if we bother to learn from them. Write down what happened, and ask yourself what elements led up to the failure? How could it have been prevented? And what more can you do the next time to prevent the same outcome? Some mistakes can be lethal, some can cost you money or friends, and some are inconsequential and could be ignored. Regardless of what type of error you made, it needs to be acknowledged and analyzed to prevent it from occurring again.

Mistakes Are Part Of Learning

Winston Churchill once said, "All men make mistakes, but only wise men learn from their mistakes." People are bound to make mistakes; it is merely inevitable. Being prepared beforehand may reduce a bit, but in the end, you cannot fully predict what may happen. It is just how it goes; people naturally cannot foretell with certainty how things will turn out. Mistakes are one impending chunk of life, which depend on many factors.

Mistakes are a way to learn, but one must admit his mistake first to learn from a mistake. It may sound easy, but for some people admitting their mistake would mean they are inferior or incompetent, which may come up with a significant blow to their ego and even their mental state.

Every person is different, so learning a lesson from mistakes would depend on the person. Some may comprehend what went wrong and then find the flaw in their doings and incarcerate it, whilst others may simply let go of it and never come back to think, what possibly went wrong and how they could learn from the mistake.

There are different types of mistakes, some arising from ignorance, some due to boredom or laziness. Another type of mistakes are the systematic mistakes; they are carved deep into your being; they are also arguably the most frustrating mistakes, hardest to overcome mistakes.

Manage Emotion

"Emotion can be the enemy, if you give into your emotion, you lose yourself. You must be at one with your emotions, because the body always follows the mind." -- Bruce Lee.

What Are Emotions?

We all are emotional people. Emotions can be positive or negative. Negative emotions play adversely to our success, whereas the positive emotion helps to boost our success. These differences are because of the varying degree of mental strength human possesses. The more the mental strength, the less impact of negative emotions in the sense that when some setback comes, our mind can convince us that this is just a setback; we should get up, learn from the mistake, and move forward to chase our goal.

Life is full of emotional highs and lows, and it plays a significant role in our success. Emotions in the form of frustration, sadness, sorrow, and disappointment discourage people from surrendering at the time of setbacks. It makes our mind think more about the negative aspects than the positive sides and ultimately prevent taking action for the goal's achievements. This happens to everybody but to varying degrees. The mentally strong people can considerably neutralize these negative emotions, but mentally weak people surrender even for little negative emotion.

How It Affects Success?

Success journey hinders or gets derailed when negative emotions attack us. Negative emotions control our minds and downplay all our positive thinking, dreams, goals, and efforts and convince our minds to accept that these goals or dreams are not achievable. This is simply a waste of time, and it is better to admit defeat and do something else.

So, what is the result? Despite the persons having all the knowledge, skills, and ability, the negative emotions stop and prevent to work for the goals and dreams.

How Mental Strength Improve Our Emotions?

Does the question arise how mentally strong people can neutralize these emotions? Mental strength is nothing but specific skills or habits to practice at the time of these setbacks. Mental strength comprises the ability to bounce back by reminding continuously that these setbacks are natural and very common in the journey of success. These setbacks remind us of our roots and reinforce our actions with more grit and determination and strengthen our actions for future goals. Negative emotions during the success journey are the blessings in disguise; we should be fully aware that these negative emotions should not spoil our goal and future success. People with high mental strength control these negative emotions and are actually able to do this.

While the short-term concealment of emotions may help certain occupations such as military personnel, police officers, and those in the medical field. Ignoring emotions is not a healthy long-term strategy. Eventually, suppressed emotions work their way out and often rear their ugly head in the form of anger. Being assertive requires an acute awareness of emotions and how those feelings can influence thoughts and behavior. Ongoing monitoring of one's emotional state helps mentally strong people control their emotions, so their emotions don't own them.

Mental strength is the key to managing your emotions. People who can manage emotions can deal with life's inevitable ups and downs effectively. Mentally stronger understand how to calm themselves down, cheer themselves up, or face their fears. Mentally strong people manage their emotions by following ways:

- Embrace discomfort: A village boy fell in a well around 7 in the evening. He tried shouting for help, but there was no one around to hear him. He had two options, swim until someone arrives or die. But that boy swam for 16 hours continuously. Being an average guy with normal physical strength, how did he make this possible? This small story indicates how mentally strong you are, depends on the situations you have been through.

  So, if you want to be mentally strong, throw yourself into difficult situations. You will be surprised to see your limits.

  In the defense and Special Forces, they do the same. They are made to go through very challenging and near-death situations just to make them mentally strong.

Many people go through life, working hard to avoid discomfort. Ironically, however, they end up feeling uncomfortable almost all the time because they're wasting all their energy running away from things that may cause discomfort. Embrace a little bit of discomfort. The more you expose yourself to uncomfortable feelings, the more you gain confidence in your ability to tolerate distress.

- Schedule a specific time for worry: One of the best ways to manage your anxious thoughts is to allot a time to worry. Set aside 20 minutes a day to worry and put it in your schedule. When you find yourself worrying outside your scheduled worrying time, remind yourself that it's not time to worry, and you'll have plenty of time to do that later.

- Check feelings: Emotions can be helpful for some and harmful to others. Sadness is helpful when it reminds you to honor something or someone you lost. But it can be harmful if it tries to keep you from getting out of bed and tackling your day.

  Anger helps give you the energy to take a stand for a cause you believe in. It can be harmful if it encourages you to do or say things that hurt people.

  Anxiety is helpful when it talks you out of doing something dangerous. But it's not helpful when it keeps you from positively stepping outside your comfort zone.

  So after you label your feelings, take a minute to identify whether that emotion is a friend or an enemy to you right now. If it's helpful, allow yourself to embrace that feeling fully. If it's not helpful, change how you feel by either changing the way you think.

- Label emotions: Labeling your feelings is key to making the best decisions. When you understand how you feel and how those feelings might cloud your judgment, you can make better choices.

  Labeling your emotions can also take the sting out of uncomfortable feelings like sadness, embarrassment, and disappointment. So check in with yourself a few times each day and identify how you're feeling.

- Engage in happiness activities: Behaving contrary to the way you feel can shift your emotional state. For example, smiling can evoke feelings of happiness when you're feeling down. Or taking a few slow deep breaths can calm you when you're feeling anxious.

  It is crucial to have a few activities in mind for boosting your mood on a bad day. The easiest way to do that is by creating a list of things you enjoy doing when you are in a good mood, like going for a walk, listening to upbeat music, or having coffee with a friend.

When you are in a bad mood, engage in something that makes you happy and relaxed. Nature has the right healing quality. So, it can be just walking alone in nature, or it can be playing with kids or reading funny books. Changing your behavior can shift your internal state and help you to feel happier.

Ultimately, mentally strong people used to follow most of the above activities to manage emotions effectively.

A young lady was waiting for her flight in the boarding room of a big airport. As she would need to wait for a long time, she decided to buy a book to read and a packet of cookies to snack on. She sat down in an armchair in the airport's VIP lounge to relax and read in peace.

A man sat down in the next seat, opened his magazine, and started reading. When she took out the first cookie, the man took one also. She felt irritated but said nothing. She just thought: “What a nerve! If I were in the mood, I would punch him for daring!”

For each cookie she took, the man took one too. This was infuriating her, but she didn’t want to make a scene. When only one cookie remained, she thought to herself, “What will this rude man do now?”

Then the man, taking the last cookie, divided it into half and offered her one part. That was too much! She was furious now. In a huff, she took her book, the rest of her things and stormed off to board the plane.

When she sat down in her seat on the plane, she looked into her purse to take out her reading glasses, and to her surprise, her packet of cookies was there, untouched and unopened.

She felt so ashamed. She realized that she was wrong. She had forgotten that her cookies were kept in her purse.

The man had divided his cookies with her, without feeling angry or bitter, while she had been outraged, thinking she was dividing her cookies with him. And now there was no chance to explain herself, nor to apologize.

Manage Stress

"Stress is caused by being 'here' but wanting to be 'there.' – ***Eckhart Tolle***

What Is Stress?

Stress is a normal part of life, and nobody is immune to stressful situations and stress. A certain amount of stress is beneficial to energies and motivates us to take action. However, stress can become a problem when it is overwhelming, and we are exposed to it for a prolonged time. Effectively coping with stress is all about finding a balance and keeping it at manageable levels.

Many things in life can lead to stress. The loss of a job, debt and financial issues, family problems, failures, relationship debacle, and demanding jobs are the causes of stress. Even positive life changes, such as moving to a bigger house, getting a job promotion, or going on holiday, can be sources of stress.

All of us can relate to at least a few of the feelings described above and felt stressed and overwhelmed at some point in time. Some people seem to be more affected by stress than others. For some people, leaving the house on time each morning can be a very stressful experience. At the same time, others may be able to cope with a great deal of pressure.

When you are stressed, you may experience many different feelings, including anxiety, fear, anger, sadness, or frustration. Managing stress is challenging to many persons, particularly for those who are not so mentally stronger. In case of any setback, their negative emotions take over and control the mind in the direction of a negative impact and its consequences resulting in stressful mental health.

When stress becomes overwhelming and prolonged, the risks for mental health problems and medical problems increase. Long-term stress increases the risk of mental health problems such as anxiety and depression, substance use problems, sleep problems, pain, and bodily complaints such as muscle tension.

How Mentally Strong People Handle Stress Effectively?

Mentally strong people know that setbacks, problems, and hardships are part and parcel of life and are inevitable, thus helping them accept stress positively and devote their efforts to move forward.

While stress causes many people to crumble, mentally strong people continue to manage flourish. In fact, they view adversity as an opportunity for self-growth. Whether they're dealing with financial setbacks, health problems, or workplace challenges, mentally strong people don't let stress drag them down.

Mentally stronger people have the ability to accept the failure, learn from the mistakes, and forget the negative emotion quickly. They show a lot of persistence and perseverance at the time of failure and can convince themselves to move forward with the task.

Mentally strong people always take inconveniences in the right perspective and positive manner. They never allow one mistake to ruin the entire day or career. They remain optimistic in such circumstances and never allow pessimistic thinking in themselves.

Amidst stressful situations, mentally strong people devote their efforts to doing what they can to move forward because they know that setbacks, problems, and hardships are inevitable. They believe that they can always take steps to improve their lives if they can’t change the circumstances.

Mentally strong people take care of their physical health as they know that they won't be able to combat stress if their health is not good. So they do physical exercise, get enough sleep, and eat nutritious foods to keep themselves fit.

Mentally strong people, however, strike the right balance in work and family life. They maintain a healthy social life even when they are stressed.

Mentally strong people acknowledge all they do, from the time they wake up until the time they go to sleep, is a choice. They are willing to say no to things they do not want to do, and they accept responsibility for their behavior.

The mentally strong people's outlook is realistic, but they look for the silver lining in challenging circumstances. They understand those good things can come up from stressful circumstances. They choose to use stressful circumstances to their advantage to become stronger and better.

Improve Performance

"Previously, I always thought it was just tactical and technique, but every match has become almost more mental than physical – I try to push myself to move well. I try to push myself not to get upset and stay positive, and that's what my biggest improvement is over all those years. Under pressure I can see things very clear." – Roger Federer

Mental strength acts as a booster to improve performance. When mental strength improves, focus improves and thereby performance and productivity. Mental strength increases the zeal and desire to work on the purpose and the goal. Mental strength eliminates or reduces distractions and increases grit and determination, and thereby improves performance.

Mental strength creates a winning mindset. When you take the example of renowned world athletes such as Roger Federer, Brian Lara, Late Mohammad Ali, Michael Phelps, and many other exceptional athletes, you will find the importance of mental toughness in creating a winning mindset. When you are mentally tough, you do not play to lose, you play to win, and your thinking is beyond the average person's mindset. As you are driven to succeed, you rise to the challenge due to the high-pressure situation. Further, mental toughness helps you create a winning mindset because it encourages you to reach your full potential. When you are working at your highest potential, you reach peak performance, which gives you the advantage to win even when you are under pressure. As you achieve more and more wins, your mindset becomes firmer and winning becomes your default thinking mode. Mentally stronger people often pride themselves on tolerating a great deal of pain and suffering, and they learn from it. Their focus is on personal growth and development.

People with high mental strength do not make any excuses when things do not go their way; instead, they always try to find a way. Instead of playing the blame game, they take responsibility for their performance, go back to the drawing board, check where things went wrong, and try again.

Instead of doing things the way they always have, mentally tough people find new ways of challenging themselves, pushing themselves to the outer limits of their potential.

Mentally strong people focus on controlling and expanding their energy on things that benefit performance. They focus on what they can do in the present moment to overcome the challenges of performance and give them the best opportunity to succeed.

Mentally tough people learn from their mistakes and others' mistakes, then they let go of the past and move forward. They see the past as mental training for better performance in the future. Mistakes, errors, and losses don’t define mentally tough athletes; these experiences strengthen their resolve.

Mentally tough people find opportunities to move out of their comfort zone and meet challenges with enthusiasm instead of anxiety. They refuse to be typecast as average and always take a chance to achieve great things.

They are very much perseverant and understand that failure is another step in the journey towards accomplishment. They have the mindset that failure is not final and never quit pursuing their objectives.

Optimal performance is a marathon, not a sprint. Each step along the way moves them closer toward the ultimate goal. They are not embarrassed by mistakes, do not try to be perfect, push themselves to the max, and seek daily improvement. Mentally tough people understand they will make mistakes along the way, and these mistakes are both necessary and critical turning points in their journey towards excellence.

Mentally strong people focus on themselves, their talents, improving themselves, implementing their game plan, and achieving the goals they set for themselves. Michael Jordan rightly said, "The mental part is the hardest part, and I think that's the part that separates the GOOD players from the GREAT players."

Improve Ones' Ability To Delay In Gratification

"The ability to discipline yourself to delay gratification in the short term in order to enjoy greater rewards in the long term is the indispensable prerequisite for success." – Brian Tracy

What do you do at the annual get-together party when you encounter platters of delicious and tempting foods when you are suffering from obesity and trying to lose weight? If you give in and fill up your plate with all mouth-watering delicacies, you will get to enjoy a bit of instant gratification, but all your efforts to lose weight will be in vain.

Benefits of Delayed Gratification

One of the most influential personal traits, followed by successful people, is delayed gratification. People who manage to delay gratification for the present moment prosper more in their professional careers, inter-personal relationships, health, and managing finances than people who give in to it. Delayed gratification is a smart way to go if you want to live a successful life in the future.

Delay in gratification is not the most effortless skill to acquire. It involves feeling dissatisfied and unhappy for the moment, so it seems impossible for people who have not learned to control their impulses. Choosing to have something now might feel good, but making an effort to have discipline and manage your impulses can result in bigger or better rewards in the future. Over time, delaying gratification improves self-control, improves the level of patience, and ultimately helps you achieve long-term goals faster.

Walter Mischel conducted a well-known experiment at Stanford University in the 1960s called The Marshmallow Experiment. In the experiment, a group of four-year-old children were placed in a room with one marshmallow on a plate and promised a second one on the condition that they wait twenty minutes before eating the first one. The experiment's idea was to see if the children who could wait would demonstrate they could delay gratification and control impulse, both significant and essential traits for attaining wealth and being financially successful. Some children were able to wait, and others could not. The researchers then followed each child's progress into adolescence and demonstrated that the children who could wait for the second marshmallow without eating the first were better adjusted and more dependable and scored significantly higher on the

Scholastic Aptitude Test years later. This shows that waiting is best, and if you learn the ways of delayed gratification, you can succeed in life.

Now, you should introspect based on the results of the study. Are you able to wait for things you want, even if it involves sacrificing pleasure and satisfaction now? Do you make decisions based on your life purpose or on what feels right now? Do you sometimes succumb to the pressure and give up too soon? Can you think of a time when you accomplished a difficult task? How did it make you feel about yourself? What were the results of waiting?

The control of temptation you exhibit when waiting for something you want says a lot about you. If you want to buy something, will you save now to pay with cash later, or pay with a credit card now and pay for it later? If you started school or own your own business and aren't seeing the rewards yet, will you keep going or give up when the going gets tough?

You are active and waiting. It calls for sacrifice now for something better later. For instance, a swimmer starts practicing swimming every morning at 5.00 a.m., when their friends are still in bed. He gives up sleep in order to win the championship next year. Delayed gratification is crucial to have a great life in the future. If a person has learned delayed gratification and can apply it to their life, they will excel in life.

In other words, delay in gratification is the act of resisting an impulse to take an immediately available reward in the hope of obtaining a more-valued reward in the future. The ability to delay gratification indicates self-regulation and self-control. This ability to resist temptation and stick to our goals is often referred to as willpower or self-control. Delaying gratification is often seen as a central part of this behavior.

Choosing a long-term reward over immediate gratification poses a significant challenge in many areas of life.

Thereby, children who learn how to delay gratification earlier in life grow up to become successful adults. The reality is that success is contingent on deferring incipient pleasure and discipline, which is the basis of delaying gratification. Without the ability to delay gratification, it is virtually inconceivable for an individual to attain success in any venture. For instance, the student who consistently chooses the immediate pleasure of watching television rather than studying for their examinations to attain a greater reward of academic achievement and possibly work success is less likely to succeed than the student who forgoes temporary pleasure to study. The weight lifter who does not discipline abstaining from tasty yet unhealthy foods is likely to score higher BMI and have a less desirable body than a disciplined weight lifter.

Instant and delayed are the two branches of gratification. People who look for instant gratification focus on the present. These people are not able to have control over their inclinations and are prone to temptations. People who search for delayed gratification will wait for the future. They maximize their pleasure by looking forward to the anticipated reward. Jake Kelfer, author and an inspirational speaker, simplified the terms by saying instant gratification is fast food on the way home. In contrast, delayed gratification is waiting to have healthier food at home, leading to a healthier and better lifestyle.

In financial language, instant gratification is getting a cash advance on a credit card. Delayed gratification is investing in mutual bonds.

Delayed gratification improves one's problem-solving skills, will power and ability to reach the goals faster. It makes a person optimistic and resilient and teaches you the benefits of hard work. Delayed gratification reinforces the value of your work. It gives self – motivation and leads to greater success in life. It improves mental health and helps to improve healthy habits. Delayed gratification has become the most compelling trait of successful people. According to Aristotle, true happiness entails delaying pleasure. A life of purpose, aligned with the seeking of true happiness, creates real joy. It keeps one's happiness meter pretty steady throughout one's life.

Methods To Improve The Mental Strength

"The strength of your mind determines the quality of your life."– Edmond Mbiaka

Be a sportsperson or entrepreneur, leader, or professionals; every person on the earth requires mental strength to succeed in life. Every human being can become mentally strong, and everyone has a scope for improvement. Mental strength is a skill that can be cultivated or developed. Going to the gym a few times will not make you physically strong; developing your mental strength is a time-consuming process and requires sincerity and discipline. Mental strength takes years to build and a lifetime to maintain. It is evident that changing your thinking pattern, feeling, and behaviors is an arduous task and require dedication and commitment.

Mental toughness is an essential trait that helps the individual perform to the best of their ability and is about knowing one's priorities at any given time and not getting distracted from them. A performer's attitude is to win or at least execute at their maximum level consistently. Their belief in themselves and their technical aptitude and training acumen is solid and unwavering.

Many people do not want to improve their lives, satisfy with life as it is. Some people are afraid of taking challenges and doing hard work, and some people doubt their ability to create positive change.

But if you want to challenge yourself to become the best in any field, increasing your mental strength will take you to the next level. Your mind can be your biggest asset or your worst enemy. When your mental strength is right, you can accomplish incredible feats.

To become mentally strong, like physical muscles, mental muscles require exercise to grow stronger. You need to do a few mental push-ups every day by challenging yourself to commit mental challenges or face your fears. Eventually, you'll build the mental strength you need to reach your most significant potential. Mental strength is developed over time by individuals who choose to make personal development a priority. As to improve physical strength, you must also give up unhealthy habits, such as eating junk food; you must develop healthy mental habits, like practicing gratitude, if we want to experience mental health gains.

You can become mentally more vigorous; the key is to keep practicing and exercising your mental muscles — just as you would if you were trying to build physical strength!

Methods to become mentally strong are very common and straightforward. But it requires years of practice to develop the mental muscle. Some of the ways are discussed below:-

- **Build Character**

  A strong character is always fearless, honest, and speaks the truth, and does not need to hide anything from others. That is why he is mentally strong and has the moral courage to face all challenges. The character is a significant factor in anybody's life. Good character is more important than health, wealth, or happiness. "When the character is lost, everything is lost" is a hundred percent true. Men of good character have been remarkably successful. Whether it was Thomas Edison, whose inventions changed the world, or Abraham Lincoln, who was president of the United States, or Gandhi, the lone crusader of nonviolence, or Mother Theresa, who chose to do social work, they were all people of character.

Everyone has character. It is your character that defines who you are and what you will become. Some people have more fully developed qualities, which set them apart from the rest. While the character has much to do with the mental and ethical traits that make a person, it actually refers to the unique qualities built into an individual's life that establish their reaction despite the circumstances.

- **Feel Grateful**

Feeling grateful makes you strong and happy. Practicing gratitude is one of the most incredible things you can do for your mental health. Gratitude helps us to keep things in perspective, even during the most challenging times. To raise a mentally strong child, you should encourage them to practice gratitude regularly. Being mentally strong means, you focus on the positives and appreciate everything in your life. Mental strength is about fully experiencing your feelings and expressing them every day. Mental toughness involves clarifying the things and people that mean the most to you and celebrating them. Cultivating a gratitude practice allows people to develop mental strength by choosing who they want to become in the future and then taking action to achieve that goal.

Make gratitude a daily habit by intentionally identifying three things in your life you are grateful for. This simple habit ensures you end each day with a feeling of accomplishment, rather than negativity. This positivity can also help build resilience.

- **Face Fears**

The only way to become fearless in pursuing your dreams and goals is to face the fear straightway. Every challenging situation that creates fear in you brings you an opportunity to overcome it and boost your confidence. If you avoid facing the fear, it becomes more extensive with time. Half of the fear vanishes if you face them and accept them. This sounds simple but requires much courage to remind yourself that you have accepted it every time. Often when we set big goals for ourselves, it is easy to get overwhelmed and be fearful of failure. In these instances, it is essential to gather up your courage and keep going, one step at a time. Most people avoid their fears; some people attempt to face the fears only to look good in front of others. But mentally strong people have nothing to prove. They confront and overcome the fears that create an updated version of themselves.

Nobody is born with unshakeable confidence. Anybody that you come across who possesses a very high level of confidence has it because they have worked tirelessly to build it.

In short, anyone can strengthen their confidence muscle. The question is, how do you practice being confident when you don’t feel like you have anything to be optimistic about?

- **Make Mistakes**

Mistakes are an inevitable part of life on the way to success. Mentally strong people are honest with themselves. Their actions never contradict their words. Moreover, they are action takers. People with mental strength dare to take action on their goals even if they don’t feel ready or feel confident. They make a mistake and move forward. Mental strength doesn't guarantee that you won't make mistakes at all. You will, but the important thing is to learn from them and move on.

Setbacks offer excellent opportunities to redirect and refocus your life, but it's up to you to set the course for the journey ahead. The next time that nothing seems to be going your way, step back, and ask yourself what the challenge is trying to teach you. This will help you prioritize your emotional health.

- **Set Goal**

The mental map of goal-setting can be used to enhance mental toughness. Goal setting gives a more profound sense of purpose. Successful people understand why achieving the goal is important and what difference it makes in one's life. This insight gives the mental toughness to take action and overcome the obstacles they may face in achieving goals. Therefore, the first step is to set the goal and believe that you can achieve it. When you set a measurable goal with a deadline, you spend time, energy, and resources to attain the goal. Having specific goals to reach desired outcomes is considered very useful.

Developing goals, making action plans to achieve these, and executing those plans requires will-power and mental resilience. Goals can be large or small, related to physical health, emotions, career, finance, spirituality.

Mental toughness only comes to life if you are working towards your goal or your target. Once you know your target, you can actively work towards achieving it.

- **Accept Change**

Life changes constantly, and sometimes it is difficult to adapt to new circumstances. Most people just try to resist those changes, but mentally strong people focus on coping with a fast-changing reality. They say that the only thing constant in life is change. As a result of difficult circumstances, specific goals may no longer be realistic or attainable. By accepting goals that you cannot change, it allows you to focus on the things that you do have control over.

- **Do Self-Talk**

Self-talk has an immense power to develop mental strength. Healthy self-talks such as thinking about personal development, action plan, improvement plans, ability, courage, and determination are very beneficial. When a person self-talk on one of the subjects, this sets some mindset and slowly develops these mindsets.

Focusing on abundance builds mental toughness. When you focus on your strengths, you build positive habits that reinforce mental strength. Feeling happy and positive reinforces self-confidence and self-esteem. Feeling negative can impact and influence your behavior making it more difficult to overcome challenges and make crucial decisions. Building the mental strength to focus on abundance requires a daily focus but can be instrumental in reaching your goals.

- **Meditate Regularly**

Based on a growing body of research, meditation shows promise in helping individuals enhance mental clarity, reduce stress, and improve self-control. Many athletes are reluctant to try meditation due to misconceptions. For those who avoid meditation because they have hyperactive minds, mindfulness meditation can be useful. With mindfulness meditation, one doesn't try to silence their thoughts. They focus on what's going on in their minds and around them while breathing deeply and being aware of thoughts but not reacting to them. It is an excellent practice for building attention and awareness, which are part of mental strength.

- **Manage Emotions**

Emotions are integral parts of the human being. Whenever there is a setback, challenges, failures, everyone shows emotions but at varying degrees. Some get very much perplexed, while some stay cool and calm and take it easy. Emotion management is nothing but how to deal with uncomfortable emotions in a better way. Children who understand their range of feelings and have experience dealing with them are better prepared to deal with the ups and downs of life.

The person with poor emotion management sharply reacts when things fall apart. Whereas the persons with the right emotion sit back, assess the situation, and take action. You can't always control how you feel. The only thing that you can control is how you respond to your feelings.

The best way to have more control over your emotional responses is to move throughout your days more mindfully. This increases the personal awareness of yourself, your experiences, and how you respond to them.

A consistent theme when investigating mental toughness is the players' ability to manage their emotions and cope with pressure. Mentally tough athletes do not merely deal with pressure, but they thrive on it and can produce an exceptional performance at crucial moments.

- **Take Ownership**

When you take ownership, it creates leverage both in the career and in life. Ownership makes a big difference in shaping your career and success. By taking ownership, individuals make continuous improvements and monitor the performance periodically instead of being complacent and sticking to the status quo. It is not prudent to wait for someone to come along and make your life better. Taking ownership helps to strengthen overall mental wellness and improves grit and determination.

You should be able to accept full responsibility for your beliefs, the way you think, work, perform and behave without blaming other people or circumstances. It is advisable not to waste valuable time and energy trying to justify why you should not be held accountable. Examine your role in executing the problem. Take time to discover exactly where you went wrong so you can use that information to improve.

- **Push One's Limit**

Many top performers find ways to push themselves and to come out of the comfort zone frequently. This helps to lay a good foundation for mental wellness. There is no more excellent teacher of confidence than to see yourself do something you avoided before.

- **Acquire Knowledge And Skills**

Acquiring knowledge and skills can play an essential part in building resilience, as it helps develop a sense of mastery and competency. Once proficiency and competency grow, people become courageous and mentally strong. Mentally strong people focus on improving their knowledge and skills at every stage of life.

- **Remain Positive**

One of the simplest ways to become mentally stronger when one is under pressure is to note what is going well. Negative or critical thoughts about oneself during a problematic situation usually only add to the mental stress. This is the opposite of what one wants.

Positive thoughts, on the other hand, increase a person's resilience to what's going on. Positive thinking, over the years, has evolved into a skill that is often misunderstood. Thinking positive means knowing when to analyze a game and be honest about what is going well. In the middle of a game, getting down on yourself and being highly critical may not be the best time or best strategy to help mental strength.

All the above methods need to be followed diligently to improve the overall mental wellness to a greater extent. Quantum of improvement depends on the consistency and the period.

Book Summary

Success breeds success. One small success motivates to go on for another success and so on. There are many pre-requisites for success. Mental strength is one of them and is considered a differentiator when a person strives to reach the top of any particular area. In general, the difference between an ordinary human being and a successful person is the level of mental strength. A country's leader is responsible for millions of individuals, and yet, most world leaders do not crumble under pressure. A leader's mental toughness is what sets him apart from ordinary folks.

It is easy to feel tough when life moves smoothly, but when inevitable challenges arise, being mentally strong will definitely equip you to deal with any problem before you. Mental strength increases your resilience to stress, improves your life satisfaction, and enhances performance. If you want to be as successful as the person you see in magazines or on television, build a success mindset where you learn how to regulate your thoughts, handle your emotions, and most importantly, behave productively regardless of any circumstance you find yourself in.

Mental toughness can help carry you through the relentless stresses and difficulties associated with managing a career and thriving in your personal life. Resilience is not an innate characteristic: it can be learned. You can become more assertive and more rigid by learning methods.

This book has elaborated the benefits of mental strength in improving courage, managing emotions, managing stress, improving confidence, and improving perseverance. Also, the concept of delay in gratification, and how it helps in bouncing back and finally, various mental strength methods to achieve the peak of the success.

"Nothing on earth can stop the man with the right mental attitude from achieving his goal; nothing on earth can help the man with the wrong mental attitude."

- Thomas Jefferson

******

Disclaimer

Although the publisher and the author have made every effort to ensure that the information in this book is correct, and while this publication is designed to provide accurate information regarding the subject matter covered, the publisher and the author assume no responsibility for errors, inaccuracies, omissions, or any other inconsistencies herein and hereby disclaim any liability to any party for any loss, damage, or disruption caused by errors or omissions, and whether such errors or omissions result from negligence, accident, or any other cause.

The ideas, procedures, and suggestions in this book are not intended as a substitute for consulting with an expert. Neither the author nor the publisher shall be liable or responsible for any loss or damage

Gratitude

This book is dedicated to my son, Swayham, whose continuous support and inspiration help me to continue on the writer's journey.

I sincerely thank the Almighty and all my readers, who inspired me with their love and appreciation for my previous books.

Jn

9 789358 113921

Printed at Repro India Ltd.